MATH
AND
LITERATURE
(K–3)

Book One

by Marilyn Burns

MATH SOLUTIONS PUBLICATIONS

Acknowledgments

Special thanks to the teachers and children in whose classes the ideas were tested.

Jill Board, Oakridge School District #76, Oregon
Ann Carlyle, Goleta Union School District, California
Joanne Downey, Tucson Unified School District (Chapter 1), Arizona
Marge Genolio, San Francisco Unified School District, California
Jody Houtz, Tucson Unified School District (Chapter 1), Arizona
Cheryl Knight, Piedmont Unified School District, California
Mary Petry-Cooper, Champaign Unit 4 School District, Illinois
Leslie Salkeld, Burlington-Edison School District, Washington
Suzanne Sheard, Tucson Unified School District (Chapter 1), Arizona
Stephanie Sheffield, Spring Independent School District, Texas
Bonnie Tank, Marilyn Burns Education Associates, California
Olga Torres, Tucson Unified School District (Chapter 1), Arizona
Lynne Zolli, San Francisco Unified School District, California

Design and production by Aileen Friedman

Copyright ©1992 by Math Solutions Publications
Reprinted August 2001

Printed in the United States of America.

ISBN 0-941355-07-1

Math Solutions Publications
A division of
Marilyn Burns Education Associates
150 Gate 5 Road, Suite 101
Sausalito, CA 94965
Telephone: (800) 868-9092 or (415) 332-4181
Fax: (415) 331-1931

www.mathsolutions.com

A Message from Marilyn Burns

We at Marilyn Burns Education Associates believe that teaching mathematics well calls for continually reflecting on and improving one's instructional practice. Our Math Solutions Publications include a wide range of choices, from books in our new Teaching Arithmetic series—which address beginning number concepts, place value, addition, subtraction, multiplication, division, fractions, decimals, and percents—to resources that help link math with writing and literature; from books that help teachers more deeply understand the mathematics behind the math they teach to children's books that help students develop an appreciation for math while learning basic concepts.

Along with our large collection of teacher resource books, we have a more general collection of books, videotapes, and audiotapes that can help teachers and parents bridge the gap between home and school. All of our materials are available at education stores, from distributors, and through major teacher catalogs.

In addition, Math Solutions Inservice offers five-day courses and one-day workshops throughout the country. We also work in partnership with school districts to help implement and sustain long-term improvement in mathematics instruction in all classrooms.

To find a complete listing of our publications and workshops, please visit our Web site at *www.mathsolutions.com*. Or contact us by calling (800) 868-9092 or sending an e-mail to *info@mathsolutions.com*.

We're eager for your feedback and interested in learning about your particular needs. We look forward to hearing from you.

A DIVISION OF MARILYN BURNS EDUCATION ASSOCIATES

CONTENTS

INTRODUCTION

Children's books are effective classroom vehicles for motivating students to think and reason mathematically. Too often, math learning is relegated to practice with textbook and workbook exercises, which cannot spark children's imagination in the ways that literature does. Incorporating children's books into math instruction helps students experience the wonder possible in mathematical problem solving and helps them see a connection between mathematics and the imaginative ideas in books.

This book describes classroom-tested ideas for linking math and literature in the primary grades. In Part 1, 10 classroom lessons using children's books are described in detail. While the lessons represent just a small sample of the book ideas we've discovered, they model the kinds of problem-solving investigations that books can initiate.

Included for each lesson are examples of children's written work. These samples are from classes in which writing was an integral part of math instruction. We've found that writing supports children's learning by helping them sort out, clarify, and define their thinking. In addition, writing helps teachers assess what students understand. It takes time, practice, and encouragement to help children comfortably describe their thinking in writing. The samples reproduced here are evidence that the payoff is well worth the effort.

Part 2 of this book presents a list of 21 additional children's books that are valuable for math lessons, with instructional ideas for each. Complete bibliographic information for all the books presented follows Part 2.

Some general suggestions for math instruction are: When posing math problems to children, give problems that either have several possible solutions or several different ways to arrive at one correct solution. Keep the emphasis of lessons on the children's reasoning processes and ask students to think about more than one way to solve a problem. Have students communicate their thinking and solutions to their classmates; hearing different approaches and seeing different solutions reinforces for children that there is more than one way to solve a problem. Encourage discussion in which students react to each other's ideas.

After reading a book, rather than presenting a problem for the class to solve, at times ask the children to come up with math problems that the book suggests. This gives children the challenge of creating as well as solving problems. Also, children's ideas can help you assess their view of problem solving in math and the sorts of problems they're comfortable with.

One caution: Remember that children don't have to do a learning activity with every book they read. Reading and enjoying books is valuable education in itself. Don't feel the need to "mathematize" books at every opportunity.

PART 1
Sample Lessons

Rooster's Off to See the World

Taught by Olga Torres

> Eric Carle's book *Rooster's Off to See the World* is about a rooster
> who one day decided that he wanted to travel. Other animals
> decided to join him. A problem arose, however, when night fell and
> they all realized that no plans had been made for food or shelter.
> Strikingly illustrated with colorful collages, the book provides a
> numerical problem-solving opportunity for young children. This
> section reports what happened in Joanne Downey's first-grade class
> at Mission View Elementary School in Tucson. Olga Torres, a
> Chapter 1 math specialist, taught the lesson.

A short while after the rooster set off to see the world, he began
to feel lonely. He met two cats and invited them to come along. They
agreed, and the three of them continued down the road.

As they wandered on, they met three frogs. Eager for company,
the rooster invited them to come along as well. In the same way, four
turtles and five fish also joined. Once the sun went down, however,
and it began to get dark, the animals all became hungry, cold, and
afraid. Unfortunately, the rooster hadn't made any plans. The story
resolves by having all the animals return home.

After reading the story, Olga asked the children to recall the animals
that had joined the rooster. She showed them the pattern of pictures
of the animals that appears on the inside front and back covers. Not
only did the pattern serve to help the children remember the
animals, it also gave Olga the opportunity to talk about the idea of
repeating patterns. Olga then asked the students to figure out how
many animals altogether set out to see the world. She gave each
child a sheet of paper on which to report their answers and show
their work. When the children had completed their solutions, Olga
asked them to explain their thinking.

Isaac had used crayons to represent the animals and showed them with tallies on his paper. "I counted the crayons," he explained, "and they made 15. I put 1 crayon, 2 crayons, 3, 4, and 5 crayons. Then I counted them altogether. I did this: 1, 2, 3, 4, 5, 6, 7, 8, 9, 10 and 5 makes 15."

Eddie drew boxes for the animals and numbered them. "I put them in boxes and counted them by 1, 2, 3," he explained.

After drawing boxes in a pattern to represent the animals, Eddie numbered them to find the total.

"I did the initials of the animals," Beverly explained. "I counted with my pencil. I came up with 15."

Stephanie kept a running total as more animals joined the group. She recorded 1, 3, 6, 10, and 15 on her paper and wrote: *15 animals went off into the world.* "I decided to add the animals," she explained.

Rafael explained how he solved the problem. "I done 1 rooster," he said, "then 2 cats, 3 frogs, 4 turtles, and 5 fish. I colored them different colors. I counted them on my hands."

Not all the children were able to get the correct answer. Sharon, for example, described what she remembered of the story. She said, "Ten animals went around the world. The rooster was first, then 2 cats and then a frog and then a turtle and a fish."

Danny got the answer of 12. He wrote: *I counted all the animals when she was reading the story.*

Phillip didn't know how to find the total. "One rooster wanted to go around the world," he said, "and then he met 2 cats. Then he said, `You want to go with me around the world?' Then 3 frogs went. Then went 4 fish and 5 turtles. I don't know the answer, but I wrote it down."

The students' papers and explanations revealed a variety of approaches and were useful for assessing the children's number understanding.

Stephanie kept a running total of the animals as they joined.

Danny was one of the children who didn't get the correct answer.

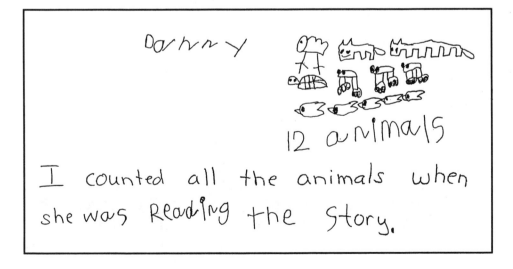

1 Hunter and One Gorilla

Taught by Jill Board and Marilyn Burns

> Both Pat Hutchins's *1 Hunter* and Atsuko Morozumi's *One Gorilla* are counting books that have children think about numbers from 1 to 10. Pat Hutchins's book is about a hunter with more determination than ability; Atsuko Morozumi's book describes animals that the author loves. The books engage children in the same sort of math investigation as *Rooster's Off to See the World,* but they extend the numbers to be added to 10. Jill Board used *1 Hunter* with first graders in Oakridge Elementary School in Oakridge, Oregon. Marilyn Burns used *One Gorilla* with second graders in Park School in Mill Valley, California.

1 Hunter

The hunter in Pat Hutchins's book stalks through the jungle with an air of determination and his rifle ready. As he walks, he passes 2 elephants, 3 giraffes, 4 ostriches, 5 antelopes, 6 tigers, 7 alligators, 8 monkeys, 9 snakes, and 10 parrots. He is observed by all of them but doesn't notice even one. The animals are curious, however, and follow him. When the hunter finally turns to take a look back, he is so terrified by the crowd of creatures he sees that he drops his rifle and flees.

This book is delightfully illustrated and gives children visual clues for guessing each group of animals before they're clearly shown.

"How many animals do you think there are altogether?" Jill asked her first graders after reading the book to them. The children paired up to find out. Jill gave each pair a sheet of unlined paper on which they were to show their work. Their papers revealed a variety of approaches for arriving at a solution.

Kyle and Thomas were partners who shared the work. On their

paper, Kyle made the dots and Thomas wrote the numbers. They counted and arrived at the correct answer of 54.

Juan and Paul listed the numbers from 10 to 2. They wrote: *We cowntid with ar fegrs.* "We counted with our fingers," they explained to Jill.

Jamie and Megan made tallies for each of the numbers from 2 to 10 and proceeded to count. However, they kept losing their place and getting confused. Finally, Jamie said, "Why don't we start from 10? I know 10 and 9 are 19." On their paper, the children explained that they counted from 19 by ones.

Stephanie and Desiree insisted on drawing the pictures of all the animals. They used three sheets of paper to complete their work. "It took them a long time," Jill wrote, "but they worked well and were happy." However, in the end they miscounted and reported an answer of 52.

The children's solutions revealed different abilities. Amber and Sarah, for example, began by drawing one of each of the animals. They wrote a number on each drawing to indicate how many of that type of animal there were in the story, and made the appropriate number of tallies next to each. Jill noticed that they had begun by correctly figuring out that there were 14 elephants, giraffes, ostriches, and antelopes altogether. But then they got bogged down and added just 1 for each of the other animals, including 1 for the hunter. They wound up with an answer of 20.

Ben and Nick organized their tallies in rows.

In contrast, Ben and Nick organized tallies in rows, labeled each row with the name of the animal, and reported that there were 54 altogether. They showed their work to Jill. "How many elephants and parrots are there altogether?" Jill asked the boys, choosing the animals from the top and bottom of their list. The boys easily figured that 2 plus 10 was 12.

"What about giraffes and snakes?" Jill continued, moving toward the middle of their list. Ben and Nick were able to add 3 and 9 easily to get 12. Jill continued with ostriches and monkeys, and the boys got 12 by adding 4 and 8. They were fascinated with the pattern.

"I wonder if that works all the time or only for the hunter book," Ben said.

The next day Ben reported to Jill that it worked for $1 + 2 + 3 + 4 + 5 + 6 + 7$. "They made 8," he said, "except a 4 was left over."

Amber and Sarah's strategy was a good idea, but their final result of 20 was not correct.

One Gorilla

One Gorilla was the 1990 winner of The New York Times Best Illustrated Children's Book Award. On the opening page, Atsuko Morozumi writes, "Here is a list of things I love." He begins with 1 gorilla, who makes his way through jungles, gardens, and forests, past 2 butterflies, 3 budgerigars, 4 squirrels, 5 pandas, 6 rabbits, 7 frogs, 8 fish, 9 birds, and 10 cats.

Marilyn showed the book to the class on the first day of school as a way of introducing them to problem solving. Also, she was interested in doing a beginning assessment of the children's number sense and their ability to represent their ideas in writing. The children enjoyed searching for the creatures and finding the gorilla on each page.

After showing the entire book to the class, Marilyn listed the numerals from 1 to 10 on the board and asked the children which animals they remembered. As students offered their ideas, Marilyn checked them in the book and wrote the names of the animals next to the appropriate numerals.

Then Marilyn posed the problem of figuring out how many animals the author loved altogether. She gave the children unlined paper on which to show their work. "You can write or draw whatever will help you think about the problem," she said. "Then write your answer and explain how you figured." To help them with their writing, Marilyn wrote on the board:

He loved __ things. I figured it by ___.

Before the children began work, Marilyn said, "Raise your hand if you understand the problem you're supposed to solve." About half the class responded. She asked them all to listen carefully and then had two children explain the problem.

"What are you supposed to write on the paper?" she asked. Again, Marilyn had volunteers explain. The class then got to work. The math period had the typical confusion of a first day at school. About half of the children were immediately engaged and went to work. Several children raised their hands for help. Several others began doing things that had nothing to do with the assignment — fiddling with things in their desk, drawing a picture that didn't relate to the problem, or wandering off to look for something. One boy had his head down and was gently sobbing, which he had been doing on and off all morning. Two boys were arguing about crayons.

As the children worked, Marilyn circulated, encouraging some

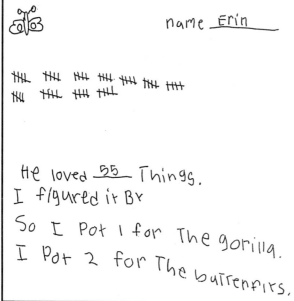

name Erin

He loved _55_ Things.
I figured it Br
So I Pot 1 for The gorilla.
I Pot 2 for The butterflrs.

Erin made tallies and then counted by 5s to find the answer.

Beau

Heloved55things,
I figured it bydots.

Beau was pleased with the pattern he made with the dots.

children, refocusing others on the task, offering help, settling disputes, pushing for more explanations, and listening to children's ideas. She tried to comfort and understand the sobbing boy, who finally lifted his head and began to draw a dinosaur on his paper. Although it had nothing to do with the book, "It's something I love," he said.

Erin found the problem easy. She made tally marks and wrote: *He loved 55 things. I figured it by so I pot [put] 1 for the gorilla. I pot 2 for the butterflys.* She left the rest to the reader's imagination. Several other children also drew lines or tally marks.

Jill was totally stuck. "These numbers are too big," she said. She had made lots of tally marks on her paper, following the lead of Erin and the others at her table, but the marks had no meaning for her. Marilyn told her that it was OK for her to explain that the numbers were too big because it was important for her to write what she really thought. Then Marilyn gave her a simpler problem to solve. She wrote on Jill's paper: *How many things can fly?* That was within Jill's reach. She wrote: *3 budgies, 9 birds, and 2 butterflys* and *3 + 9 + 2 = 14.*

Daniel listed the numbers on his paper in the following order: *10, 9, 1, 8, 2, 7, 3, 6, 4, 5.* He wrote: *He loved 55 things. I added together to make 10s and then I added a 5. I did it in my head.*

Beau drew dots in a triangular pattern, with 1 in the top row, 2 in the second row, and continuing to a tenth row with 10 dots in it. He was pleased with the pattern and showed it to the others at his table, inspiring some of them to do the same. He wrote: *He loved 55 things. I figured it by dots.* Several other children had also drawn dots.

Finally, Marilyn called all the children together and asked for volunteers to share their solutions. In this way the children had the chance to hear others' solutions and could see a variety of ways to organize their work on their papers.

He loved 55 things. I added together to make 10,s and then I added a 5, I did it in my head.

10
9
1
8
2
7
3
6
4
5

Combining 10s allowed Daniel to figure in his head.

17 Kings and 42 Elephants

Taught by Jody Houtz and Suzanne Sheard

Margaret Mahy's book *17 Kings and 42 Elephants* describes a royal procession through an exotic jungle. Mahy's infectiously rhythmic language is matched by Patricia MacCarthy's animated batik illustrations. The book is a total delight and has become a favorite in all classes in which it has been introduced. The work shown is from Jody Houtz's class in Van Buskirk Elementary School and Suzanne Sheard's class in Drachman Primary Magnet School, both Chapter 1 third-grade classes in Tucson Unified School District.

Seventeen kings on forty-two elephants
Going on a journey through a wild wet night,
Baggy ears like big umbrellaphants,
Little eyes a-gleaming in the jungle light.

So begins the journey in Mahy's book. The procession of kings and elephants rollicks and sways past crocodiles, tigers, cranes, peacocks, gorillas, flamingos, baboons, and more. The rich language transports children to a mysterious paradise and delights them with captivating tongue-twisters.

After hearing the story twice, the students were asked to solve the problem of how 17 kings could share the work of caring for 42 elephants. Children were asked to talk about the problem with their partners but to write individual solutions. They were asked to write all they could to explain what they did.

The children took different approaches. Jolene drew 17 kings and 42 elephants and wrote: *All the kings will have 2 elafant and thar will be 8 left. I crost off one king and one elafant and thean I had some left. so I pout 2's on the kings and then I had some left and they what [went] to the zoo.*

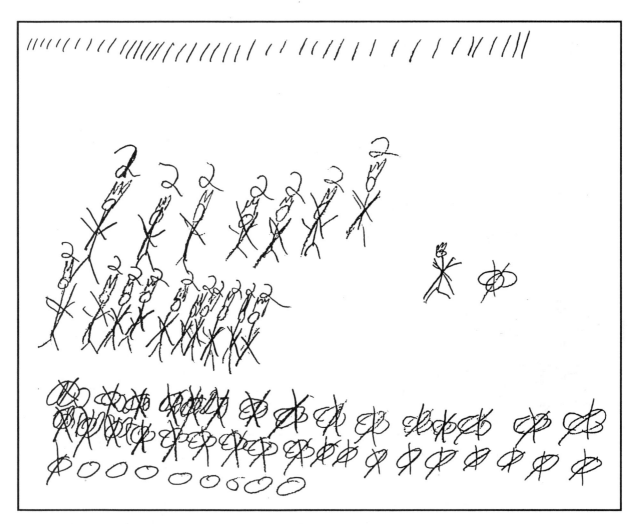

Jolene's work shows how she divided the elephants among the kings.

Lori Ann drew 17 circles, put 2 tally marks in each to represent the elephants, and wrote *R8* to indicate the remainder. She wrote: *Each king got two elephants.* She also drew a picture, which she captioned: *Elephants for sale, 600.00 dollers each.*

Some children used calculators. Desiree, for example, drew a picture of a calculator and wrote: *I used the calculator. I put 42 minus 17 = 25 miness 17 = 8. Each king gets 2 elephant. The 8 left elephants cood be shared with the people.*

Claudia had a different suggestion for the extra elephants. She wrote: *17 kings can have 2 elephants and the rest can go bak to the pales* [palace]. *8 can be left at the pales.*

Manny had a completely different idea and wound up with extra kings instead of extra elephants. He wrote: *1 on 3 elephants and the wrest of the kings have to walk.*

Lori Ann took an entrepreneurial approach to dealing with the extra elephants.

Crista's illustration shows her idea for coaxing an elephant to walk.

Joey suggested a system of merit pay. He wrote: *I think that eight of the most goodest kings' will get three elepants' togeter with ropes and all the other kings' will get 2 elepants' and their was nine king's had two elphants'.*

Crista wrote: *the kings has to have 2 each and they can tren* [train] *the rest and they kings will have a good toldol* [total]. Her illustration showed a king riding an elephant, holding a long rod that had a peanut dangling off the end. Crista's idea was that the peanut would coax the elephant to keep walking.

Ethan added 17 and 17, got 34, and then counted on to 42 in order to figure out there were 8 elephants left. He drew fingers to show how he counted.

Timothy used cubes to make the problem more concrete. He wrote: *I think each king shod get 2 elephants. I tok 1 unifix cubes for each king and 2 unifix cubes for an elephant. One king gets 2 elephant. You hav 8 elephants left.*

Joey suggested a system of merit pay for kings who performed well. His writing shows his interest in, and confusion with, the use of the apostrophe.

The children in both classes spent more than an hour working on the problem. The variety of solutions is a tribute to children's inventiveness and to the uniqueness of their thinking. Although not all the students arrived at the correct answer, all were engaged in thinking mathematically.

Note: In some classes in which this book was used, students were first told to think about what sorts of math problems could be asked. In this way, the children could create as well as solve problems. The suggestions we received included the following:

How many footprints did they all make in the jungle?

How many ears and tails did they have altogether?

How many more elephants than kings were there?

Ten Black Dots

Taught by Olga Torres and Marge Genolio

In *Ten Black Dots*, Donald Crews uses black dots in colorful illustrations of everyday objects. He begins with 1 dot and continues up to 10 dots. Simple rhymes accompany the graphics. The work in this section was done near the end of the school year by Marge Genolio's first graders in Jefferson School in San Francisco. Marge got the idea for the project from Olga Torres, who introduced the book to first graders in Mission View Elementary School in Tucson.

Donald Crews begins *Ten Black Dots* with a question: "What can you do with ten black dots?" The book continues:

*One black dot can make a sun
or a moon when day is done.
Two dots can make the eyes of a fox
or the eyes of keys that open locks.*

Marge read the book several times to her first-grade class and then asked the children for their ideas about what to do with 1, 2, 3, and on up to 10 black dots. The children had many suggestions, and Marge gave all who had ideas the opportunity to share them. She then suggested that they each make their own "Ten Black Dots" books. The children were interested and eager.

Marge bought two packages of 3/4-inch black adhesive dots from a stationery store and brought them to class. She also provided a supply of paper to be used for the books — newsprint with an unlined top portion for illustrations and a lined bottom portion for the children's writing. The students worked on their books over a period of time; most completed one or two pages each day. Marge collected the books as they were finished and, over several days, had children share what they had created.

After all the children had presented their work, Marge showed the class the two packages of dots she had bought and the dots that remained. She told the class that a full package had 1000 dots and pointed out that some dots were left over.

"How many dots do you think the class used?" she asked the children. Some children guessed. Others had no idea. One child suggested they could use a calculator to find out, and many of the others thought that was a good idea.

Marge then said, "Let's start by figuring out how many you each used to make your book." Marge told them they could use any materials they would like to help them figure out the answer. To help them in reporting their results, she wrote on the board:

We each needed __ dots. I got my answer by _____.
Marge asked them to copy what she had written, record their answer, and explain their reasoning.

Nine of the children arrived at the correct solution of 55. Their explanations, however, differed. Carla wrote: *I got my answer by 1 + 2 + 3 + 4 + 5 + 6 + 7 + 8 + 9 + 10 = 55.* Linda wrote: *I got my answser by counting by one.* Keenahn wrote: *I got the answer by counting the dots in my book.* Diana wrote: *I got my answer by unfix qub.* Adam wrote: *I got my answer by uozing tale marks.*

Carla's solution shows her comfort with numerical representation of the problem.

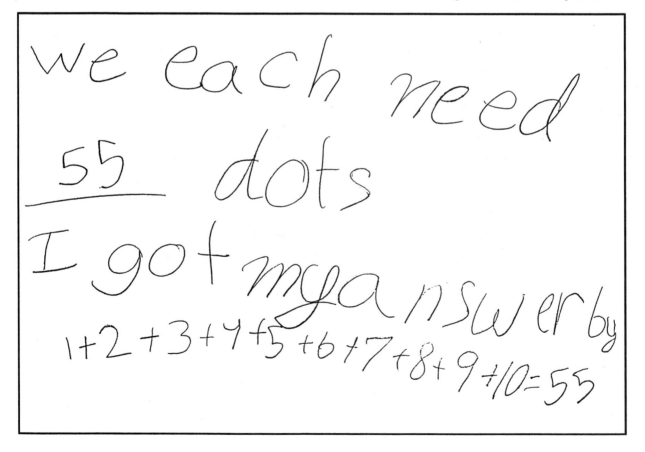

Linda

We each needed 55 dot

I got my answer by couing

Linda's drawing helped her figure out the number of dots each child needed.

Adam found tally marks useful for figuring out the answers.

Adam

~~|||| |||| |||| |||| |||| |||| |||| |||| |||| |||| |||~~

We each needed 55 dots

I got my answer by uozing tale-maks.

Children had many different ideas for incorporating dots into illustrations.

Nine dots can make nine rabbit.

Some children used reasonable approaches but got the wrong answer because of a calculation error. William, for example, drew marks in orderly clusters, beginning with 1 mark and continuing to 10. However, he left out a cluster of 7, and also miscounted what he drew. He wrote: *We each needed 38 dots.* Shirley added the numbers from 1 to 10 and got an answer of 50. Stephanie drew pictures of the dots in a carefully arranged pyramid and reported: *We each need 53.* Nicole also got an answer of 53. She wrote: *I got my answer by used unafix xubes.*

For some children, the numbers were too confusing. Lety wrote: *We think we need 19 dots because we need more than ten. When we were on the eight page we had more then ten.* Michala wrote: *We each needed 15. I gastht* [guessed]. Kenneth wrote: *We each needed 10 dots.* He didn't offer any explanation.

For students who finished quickly and were interested in more, Marge offered the problems of figuring how many dots were used altogether by everyone in the class or by all the children at their table. Five children worked on the problem. Alice explained that she used a calculator. She wrote: *Our class needed 1450 dots. Our table needs 330 dots. I got my answer by yousing the caokyoulether.* Keenahn wrote: *55 x 28 = 1540. Our clas needs 1540 dots. 55 x 6 = 330. Our table needs 330 dots. I got my answers by multeplying.*

Five dots can make a caterpillar

Four dots can make water dropping out of a foucet

The range of abilities in Marge's class is not unusual for a class of first graders — or for a class at any grade level. A problem such as this one is useful for assessing what students can do with numbers and how they think. Students need many such problems to help develop number sense, to learn ways to compute, and to become aware that there are more ways than one to solve a problem.

Two Ways to Count to Ten

Taught by Bonnie Tank

Two Ways to Count to Ten is a Liberian folktale retold by Ruby Dee. The story promotes the idea that it's not always the biggest or strongest but sometimes the cleverest who wins the prize. The story is about the leopard's search for an animal to marry his daughter and rule the jungle after his death. Bonnie Tank read the book to a class of second graders in Jefferson School in San Francisco and then involved the children in investigating number patterns.

King Leopard gathered the animals of the jungle into a huge circle and explained how he would choose his successor. He flung his spear high into the air and said, "He who would be our prince must also throw the spear toward the sky. He must send it so high that he can count to ten before it comes down again."

The elephant stepped forward to try first, but he failed. So did the bush ox, the chimpanzee, and the lion. Finally, the antelope succeeded. He flung the spear far up into the air, and before it returned to earth, he called out five words, "Two! Four! Six! Eight! Ten!"

After reading the story, Bonnie asked the children if they could think of any other ways to count to 10. Children had some suggestions. "5, 10." "1, 2, skip a few, 10." "10, like in 10, 20, 30." On the board, Bonnie listed the different ways to count to 10.

> *1, 2, 3, 4, 5, 6, 7, 8, 9, 10*
> *2, 4, 6, 8, 10*
> *5, 10*
> *1, 2, skip a few, 10*
> *10*

Ways to count to 48

1. 1,2 skip a lot 48.
2. 1,2,3,4,5,6,7,8,9,10,11,12,13,14,15,16,17,18,19,20,21,22,23, 24,25,26,27,28,29,30,31,32,33,34 35,36,37,38,39,40,41,42,43, 44,45,46,47,48.
3. 2,4,6,8,10,12,14,16,18,20,22,24,26,28,30,32,34,36,38,40, 42,44,46,48.
4. 8,16,24,32,40,48.
5. 6,12,18,24,30,36,42,48.
6. 4,8,12,16,20,24,28,32,36,40,44,48.
7. 48.

Eric listed the 7 ways he found to count to 48.

She talked with the children about the number patterns and then asked, "What if the king had given the challenge of counting to 12 instead of 10?" As the children volunteered different ways, Bonnie recorded them on the chalkboard. She was surprised that some children were able to count by threes and fours, as she didn't expect second graders to be able to do so.

                1, 2, 3, 4, 5, 6, 7, 8, 9, 10, 11, 12
                2, 4, 6, 8, 10, 12
                1, 2, skip a few, 12
                6, 12
                3, 6, 9, 12
                4, 8, 12

The children's interest was high, so Bonnie continued by having them think about different ways to count to 14.

Bonnie then posed a different problem. "The antelope won by counting by twos," she began, "but suppose the king picked a larger number. How would the antelope know whether counting by twos would work?"

In response, some children volunteered other numbers for which counting by twos would work. Bonnie listed their suggestions on the board and had the children test them aloud. Several children noticed that all the numbers listed were even.

"So the antelope would know that if the number was even, counting by twos would work," Bonnie concluded. It was then time for recess. On her way out, Cynthia came to Bonnie to explain her discovery. "I can count to 9 by twos," she said, "1, 3, 5, 7, 9." So much for Bonnie's generalization!

Several days later, Bonnie returned to the investigation. She read the book aloud again, and the children were just as interested as they had been the first time.

"Suppose the king wanted to choose a harder number," Bonnie asked the class. "What number might he choose?"

One child suggested 20 and another suggested 100. "Let's try an in-between number," Bonnie said. "Let's figure out all the ways there are to count to 48."

The children worked individually but consulted with each other. A few asked Bonnie for number charts, and she made 0-99 charts available to the entire class.

Children worked differently and displayed their work differently. Some listed the numbers they could count by, while others also

Maria described her reasons for each of the 9 ways she found to count to 48.

9 Ways to count to 48
You can count to 48 by 2's because 48 is an even number. You can count by 1's. You can count by 24's. You can count by 4's because there's a 4 in 48. You can count by 3's. And by 6's. And by 1,2, Skip a few. And you can count by 12's because of you add 12 4 times you'll come up with 48. And by 48's.

included numbers that didn't work. Some added or counted on their fingers to figure, while others used the number charts to help. Some tested numbers in an orderly sequence, while others experimented with numbers in random order. All the children were interested and involved.

KC listed 10 ways to count to 48, as well as 8 numbers that he thought wouldn't work.

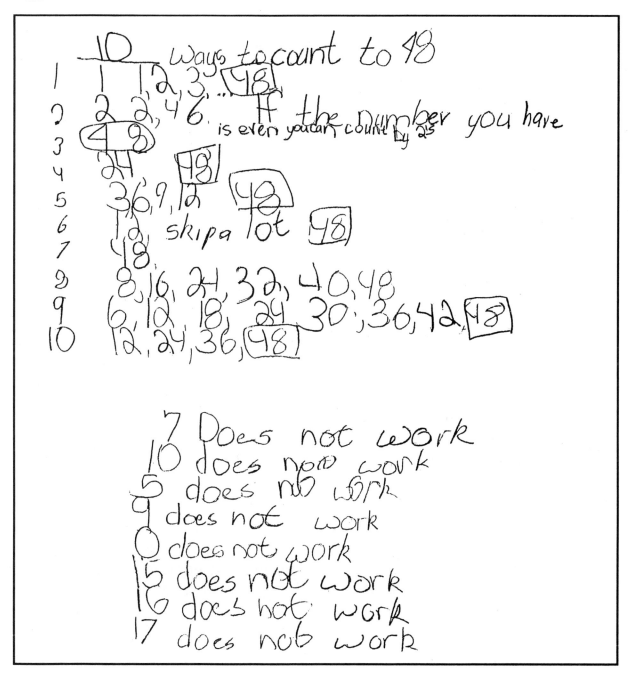

A Three Hat Day

Taught by Bonnie Tank and Marilyn Burns

Laura Geringer's book *A Three Hat Day* is ideal to read to young children. Delightfully illustrated by Arnold Lobel, the book tells the story of R. R. Pottle the Third, a man who truly loved hats. Bonnie Tank read the book to a class of first graders at Wildwood School in Piedmont, California, and then used the story to involve the children in a problem-solving math lesson. Marilyn Burns did a similar lesson with a third-grade class in Park School in Mill Valley, California.

R.R. Pottle came from a family of collectors. His father collected canes and his mother liked umbrellas. Together they took long walks in the rain.

After his parents died, R. R. Pottle lived alone. At times, however, he was very lonely. One day, to cheer himself up, he put on three of his hats — a bathing cap, a fire helmet, and a sailor hat — and went for a walk.

On his walk, R. R. happened upon a hat store and made the acquaintance of the woman who owned it. Their common interest in hats drew them together. They fell in love, married, and had a child, R. R. Pottle the Fourth. (It turns out that R. R. Pottle the Fourth didn't like hats, umbrellas, or canes. She loved shoes.)

Results from First Graders

After reading and discussing the story, Bonnie asked, "Which hat did R. R. Pottle put on first?" She showed the children the cover illustration from the book, and the children were able to figure out which hat R. R. had put on first, second, and then last.

Bonnie then presented a problem for the children to solve. "Suppose R. R. Pottle wanted to cheer himself up on another day with the same three hats," Bonnie said, "but he decided to put on the hats in a different order. And then the next day he put them on in a different order again. The problem for you to solve is to figure out how many days R. R. Pottle could wear those same three hats if each day he wanted to wear them in a different order."

Bonnie talked to the children about how they were to work. "You'll each work with a partner," she said. "Think about what can help you solve the problem. You may want to use cubes for the hats, you may want to use pictures, or you may decide that symbols are helpful. What do I mean by symbols?"

Some of the children had ideas. "Like a drawing?" Robert asked.

"Yes, that's one idea," Bonnie answered. "Does anyone have another idea?"

"Maybe letters," Kimberly said.

"That's another idea," Bonnie said. "What letter might you use for the fire helmet?" In unison, several children suggested *F*. They talked about using *B* and *S* for the other two hats.

When they got to work, all the children were engaged in solving the problem. It seemed to be just right for the first graders — challenging, interesting, and possible.

Laura and Sammy used drawings to represent their solution.

Kimberly and Joanna started by drawing hats and then switched to symbols.

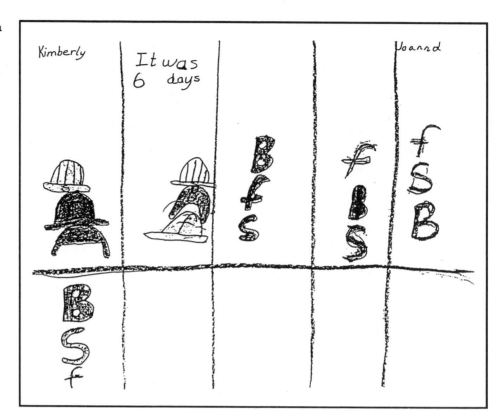

Robert and Tim defined their numerical code for the hats.

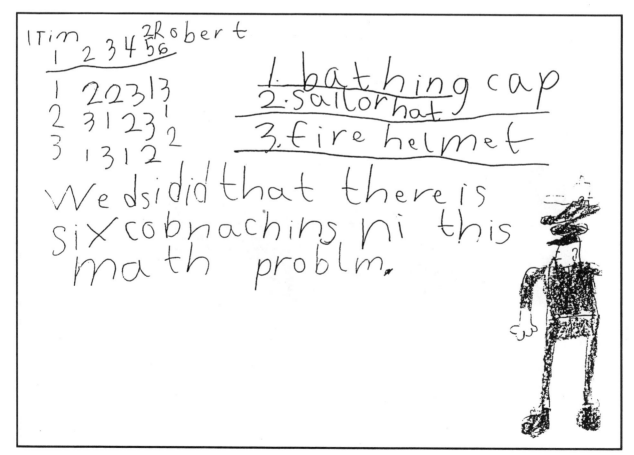

We got 5 wa

Thayer and Ashleigh drew portraits of R. R Pottle, each with a different arrangement of hats.

Results from Third Graders

The problem was just as suitable for third graders. Marilyn presented the problem the same way Bonnie had presented it to the first graders, but she extended it in several ways.

As children completed their solutions, Marilyn gave them the challenge of figuring out how many different ways R. R. Pottle could wear four hats, suggesting that they use a top hat for the fourth hat. Half of the 19 children who had time to try this challenge solved it correctly. On their own, 2 children extended the problem to five hats.

When Marilyn read the students' papers after class, she noticed that children took different approaches to find all the permutations of hats. She decided to do a follow-up lesson so the children could see

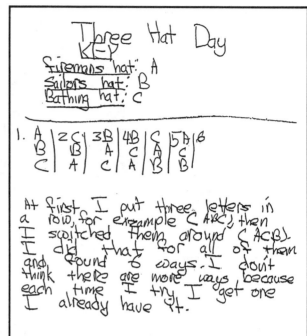

Jenee wrote 2 solutions for each hat on the top and 2 for each hat on the bottom. Then she eliminated duplicates.

Rebecca used trial and error to find the 6 arrangements.

the different ways they reasoned. It's important for children to realize that problems can be solved in many different ways.

Marilyn focused on the children's work for the three-hat problem and looked for papers that had two kinds of differences — in the symbols the children used to represent the hats and in the system they used to be sure they had found all the possible arrangements. She chose seven children's papers and, using a separate large sheet of paper for each, wrote the first three items of each solution.

The next day, Marilyn gathered the children together and began by showing them what she had copied from Sam's paper. Sam had used the letter *A* for the fireman's hat, *B* for the shower cap, and *C* for the sailor cap. He had listed the following:

A	A	B
B	C	C
C	B	A

"What do you think Sam wrote next?" Marilyn asked the class.

About half the children raised their hands. Marilyn called on Brian. "It would be *B A C*," he said, and then explained, "because he started with *A* two times and then switched to *B*." Marilyn confirmed Brian's idea and added it to the list.

Melina's display page shows that she had anticipated more solutions. Her explanation reveals that she figured out why there were only 6 arrangements.

```
A     A     B     B
B     C     C     A
C     B     A     C
```

"What do you think Sam wrote next?" she asked. All the children knew that he started with *C,* but there was disagreement as to whether he had written *C B A* or *C A B.* Marilyn acknowledged that both suggestions were possible. "Sometimes you don't have enough information to predict positively what comes next," she said. She told them what Sam had written next, and they then knew his last entry.

Marilyn repeated this sort of discussion for several other children's work. Andy, for example, had used a rotating system. His first three permutations were as follows:

```
BC     SC     FC
FC     BC     SC
SC     FC     BC
```

Marilyn also showed two solutions with randomly ordered arrangements. She wanted to give children the chance to see how patterns made it easier to predict beyond the information that is available.

Lisa found all 24 ways and explained her method.

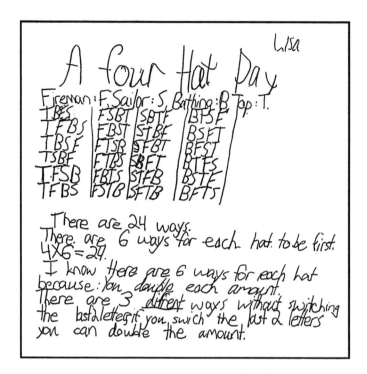

Leif repeated the same 6 arrangements for 3 hats and inserted the new hat in 4 different positions.

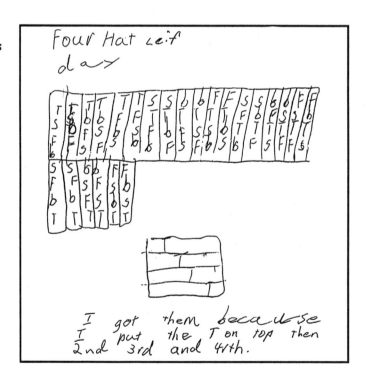

"Smart"

Taught by Cheryl Knight

Where the Sidewalk Ends, Shel Silverstein's book of poems, is a favorite for many children. Cheryl Knight read the poem "Smart" to her class of second and third graders in Wildwood School in Piedmont, California. The poem tells the story of a boy who started with a one dollar bill and made several exchanges for coins. For a math problem-solving homework assignment, Cheryl asked the children to think about and comment on the boy's understanding of money.

Smart

My dad gave me one dollar bill
'Cause I'm his smartest son,
And I swapped it for two shiny quarters
'Cause two is more than one!

And then I took the quarters
And traded them to Lou
For three dimes — I guess he don't know
That three is more than two!

In the next three verses of the poem, the boy continues trading — for 3 dimes, then for 4 nickels, and finally for 5 pennies. The final verse explains the boy's understanding of his father's reaction:

And then I went and showed my dad,
And he got red in the cheeks
And closed his eyes and shook his head —
Too proud of me to speak!

Kostas used the
example of a $1000
bill to explain his
reasoning.

Q: Did the boy get a good deal like he thought he did? NO

Explain why. (use the back if you need to.)
He did not get a good deal because every time he traded he got more coins and less value. It's better to have a 1000 — doller bill than 1000 pennies.

Cheryl Knight assigns math homework to give her students additional opportunities to think and reason mathematically. Also, she feels it's beneficial to involve parents with their children's learning at home. At back-to-school night, Cheryl discusses her homework policy and gives parents guidelines for working with their children. She asks them to take interest, be encouraging, listen to their children's ideas, and ask questions rather than tell answers.

After reading "Smart" to her class, Cheryl discussed the poem with the children. She then told them that, for homework, they were to think further about the boy's ideas. Cheryl reproduced the poem for the children and wrote a question for them to answer: *Did the boy get the good deal he thought he did? Explain why.*

The children's papers contained a variety of explanations. Anne, a second grader, wrote: *No, because he is trading coins, and for instance, three is more than two. but if he traded like this: 1 dollar for two dollars that would be better. He got more coins, but less money.*

Victoria, also a second grader, wrote: *No. He was useing sense. But then again he wasn't. A Dollar is more than 50¢. 50¢ is more than 30¢ and so on and when he comes to 5 pennies he thinks he's smart but is he? No.*

Q: Did the boy get a
good deal like he
thought he did?
Explain why. (use the
no back if you need to.)
NO

no because he is
trading coins and
for instance, three
is more than two,
but if he traded
like this: 1 dollar for
two dollars that
would be better.
He got more
coins, but less

money.

Anne explained why the boy got more coins but
less money.

Q: Did the boy get a
good deal like he
thought he did?
Explain why. (use the
back if you need to.)

Sometimes
more
is
Less
and
Less
is
more.

Bert wrote a terse answer.

Another second grader, Lauren, developed her argument in detail.
She wrote: *No. Because 2 is more then 1 but 50¢ is less then $1.00.
And 3 is more then 2 but 30¢ is less then 50¢. And 4 is more then 3
but 20¢ is less then 30¢. Also 5 is more then 4 but 5¢ is less than
20¢. So, Lou, Old Blind Bates, and Hiram Coombs are all smarter
then that fool boy!*

Zach, a third grader, wrote a lengthy explanation. He wrote: *no he
did not get a good deal because his Dad gave him a dollar. And
he traded it for two quarters but a dollar is a hudred pennies and*

two quarters is 50 pennies. Then he traded them again for three dimes and three dimes is only 30 pennies. Then he traded those and got four nickels and four nickels is 20 pennies. Then he traded those for five pennies and five pennies is a nickel. And so he got five pennies instead of 100 pennies.

Another third grader, Kostas, showed his understanding of a larger denomination of money. He wrote: *He did not get a good deal because every time he traded he got more coins and less value. It's better to have a 1000-doller bill than 1000 pennies.*

Bert, also a third grader, gave a terse answer: *Sometimes more is less and less is more.*

Little House in the Big Woods

Taught by Mary Petry-Cooper

> Mary Petry-Cooper was reading *Little House in the Big Woods* by
> Laura Ingalls Wilder to her third graders in Dr. Howard School in
> Champaign, Illinois. A situation described in Chapter 10 presented
> a math problem for her class to solve. Mary used the activity as a
> springboard for further teaching of fractions.

Chapter 10 of the book takes place in summer, a time when
people often went visiting. Sometimes, Ma would let Laura and Mary
visit Mrs. Peterson, a neighbor. At the end of their visits, Mrs.
Peterson always gave each of the girls a cookie. And the girls
always considered how to share the cookies with Baby Carrie.

*Laura nibbled away exactly half of hers, and Mary nibbled
exactly half of hers, and the other halves they saved for Baby
Carrie. Then when they got home, Carrie had two half-cookies, and
that was a whole cookie.*

*This wasn't right. All they wanted to do was to divide the cookies
fairly with Carrie. Still, if Mary saved half her cookie, while Laura
ate the whole of hers, or if Laura saved half, and Mary ate her
whole cookies, that wouldn't be fair, either.*

*They didn't know what to do. So each saved half, and gave it to
Baby Carrie. But they always felt that somehow that wasn't quite fair.*

Mary asked her third graders to think about the problem. "The
children really identified with Laura and Mary and their cookie
dilemma," Mary observed. "I was intrigued with the variety of
solutions the children generated."

Most of the children suggested a way of dividing the cookies into
parts. Their particular methods, however, differed. Several children
divided each cookie into three parts so that Laura, Mary, and Baby

Allison

How to Split Cookies

If you had 3 Kids and two cookie and did not no how to devide them heres how to do it: Devide the 2 cookies in to three part and then you would have 2 pieces for everybody.

Allison divided each cookie into thirds.

Terri's solution shows halves and sixths.

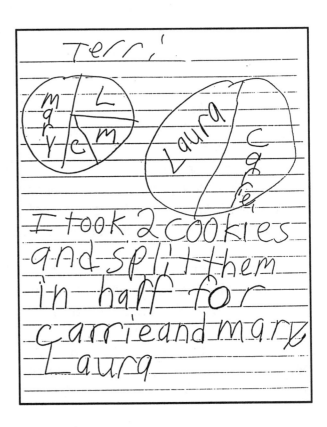

Terri

I took 2 cookies and split them in half for carrie and mary Laura

Jason divided each cookie into nine pieces and gave six to each child.

Carrie would get two pieces each. Allison, for example, wrote: *If you had 3 kids and two cookie and did not no how to devide them heres how to do it: Devide the 2 cookies into three part and then you would have 2 pieces for everybody.*

Three children divided each cookie into nine segments and labeled six for each child. Jason, for example, wrote: *They could split the cookies like a pizza. So they all could get six.*

Terri divided both cookies into halves and labeled one half for each of the three children. She then divided the remaining half into thirds and labeled each part. She wrote: *I took 2 cookies and split them in half for carrie and mary and Laura.*

Clinton described the
situation and then
presented his
solution.

Clinton S.

3rd grade

How Two Split Cookies in The Olde'n Days

This problem circles around 3 young girls named Laura, Mary, and Carrie in the book Little House in the Big Woods. In one part of the story they me'et a Swed-ish woman named Mrs. Pete-son. She gave Laura and Mary one cookie once a week. But baby Carrie needs to have a least a little bit of a cookie. My class didn't think the way the cookies were devided was fair. Here is how I made it better:

C=Carrie M=Mary L=Laura

Ashley divided each cookie into fourths and labeled one part of each cookie for company. She wrote: *I think they should divide them into 4s. Then save the other two for company. But only if there's two people for company.*

Clinton wrote a long description of the story and then showed how to divide each cookie into sixths. He labeled four sections for each child.

Some children, however, didn't divide the cookies but instead found social solutions to the problem. Antonio, for example, wrote: *They should save them an tale* [until] *there are six cookies so it will be evon.*

Chris's solution was brief and direct. He wrote: *Ask for three cookies, one for Carrie.*

Timika was a bit more politic in a similar suggestion: *When you go to some bodys house and they give you and somebody else who went with you a cookie and you had a younger you can ask for another one.*

Melanie's idea was more expansive. She wrote: *Ask the little lady to give them five cookies one for mom for dad for carrie for mary and for lura.*

Mary planned to follow this problem with others that would focus her students on fractions.

The Button Box

Taught by Bonnie Tank

> *The Button Box*, by Margarette S. Reid, is a delightful invitation to the pleasures of a button collection. To a little boy with a vivid imagination, his grandmother's button box holds more than buttons. Bonnie Tank read the book to a kindergarten class and engaged the children in several days of activities in which they sorted, counted, described, and compared buttons.

*T*he Button Box is about a little boy who is fascinated and entertained by his grandmother's button collection. He imagines where the buttons came from and the clothes they once adorned. His grandmother plays sorting games with him and tells stories about what some of the buttons used to be. The book ends with a brief history of buttons.

Bonnie read the story and the history of buttons to the class. "Who has a button collection at home?" she asked. Many hands were raised.

"Can anyone describe the container that holds your buttons?" Bonnie then asked.

"We have a button box," Cynthia said, "but it's like a rectangle, not a circle like the one in the book."

"Our buttons are in a can," Paul said. "It's taller than the one in the book."

Other children also described their containers. Bonnie suspected that several of the children described imaginary button boxes that had lids with hinges and locks and keys. It was clear that some of the children thought of button collections as real treasures.

"Is anybody wearing buttons today?" Bonnie asked.

There were seven children with buttons, and Bonnie asked them to come to the front of the class. The class counted how many buttons each child had. Devin noticed that four people had two buttons. Charles commented that Emma had the most.

After the seven children were seated, Bonnie told the students they were going to start a class button collection. She asked that each child bring one button to school. To help them remember, and to give parents information, Bonnie sent home the following note along with an envelope for the button.

Dear Parents,

After discussing Margarette S. Reid's book *The Button Box* in class, the children have become interested and curious about buttons. I've asked the children each to bring a button to school for our class button collection. We will be doing a variety of math activities that will engage the children in sorting, comparing, and counting buttons. Please send a button you no longer need.

Thank you,

Bonnie brought extra buttons to add to the class collection; that way, any child who didn't bring a button could participate. To begin the class exploration of buttons, Bonnie had the children sit in a circle on the rug and put their buttons in front of them. "I wonder if any of the buttons are the same," Bonnie said.

The children noticed that several students had brought white buttons. Upon closer inspection, they noticed the differences — some had two holes and some had four, some were small and some were big. The children also made other observations, that Jenny had brought a button shaped like a heart, for example, and that Georgia's button was shiny and looked like a flower.

Bonnie then had the children work in pairs to compare their buttons. She chose Lea for a partner and modeled for the children what they were to do. Bonnie made the first observation. "My button is red and Lea's is green," she said. Lea said, "Mine has two holes and yours has four."

"With your partner," Bonnie said, "take turns telling something that is the same or different about your buttons." After giving them a few minutes to compare buttons in pairs, Bonnie had a class discussion in which children reported what they had noticed about their buttons.

Bonnie collected the buttons by playing a game. She gave directions such as, "Button, button, who has a button that's not white?"

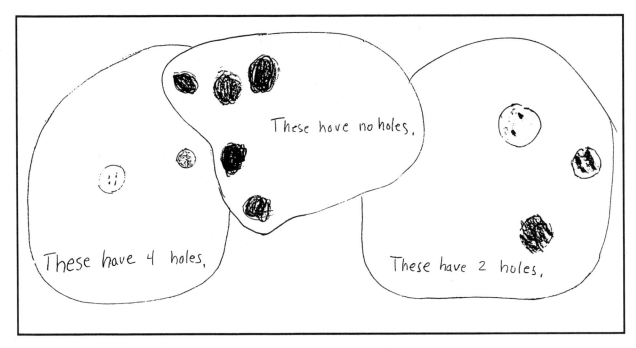

These have no holes.

These have 4 holes.

These have 2 holes.

Rory and Lisa sorted their buttons into three groups.

and "Button, button, who has a button that's round?" When a description fit, children deposited their buttons in the cookie tin that one of the parents had donated. Bonnie added the buttons she had brought.

The following day, Bonnie taped a sheet of chart paper on the front board and had the class gather on the rug. She taped two buttons next to each other at the top of the chart.

"Who can tell something that's either the same or different about these two buttons?" Bonnie asked. As the children provided information, Bonnie recorded what they said on the chart:

One button looks like butterscotch.
One is big and one is little.
One has two holes and one has four.
The buttons are different colors.
One is white and one is orange.
The buttons are both round.
The white one looks like a plate.
They both have a bump. One bump is outside and one is inside.
One is thick and one is not.
One is wide and one is not.

The next day, Bonnie again had the children sit in a circle on the rug. She had a sheet of 12-by-18-inch newsprint, the button box, crayons, and a spoon to demonstrate the activity they would do that day. "You and your partner will use one sheet of paper," Bonnie began. "First you'll fold your paper in half and write your names." Bonnie demonstrated how to fold the paper and, with Weslie as her partner, showed how they would write their names on different halves of the paper.

"Then I'll come around and put a spoonful of buttons on your paper," Bonnie continued. She put a spoonful on the sheet of paper she shared with Weslie, trying to keep the number of buttons between 10 and 14.

"Your job is to sort them in different ways," Bonnie said. "You tell one thing about the buttons, and then sort them into two sets. Let's try it with the buttons Weslie and I have. Who notices one thing about some of the buttons?"

"Some are white," Georgia said.

"On one half of the paper," Bonnie said, "put the buttons that are white. The rest go on the other side." Several of the children sitting nearby helped. Then Bonnie asked the children for other ways to sort the buttons, and they did so several more times.

"Finally," Bonnie said, "you and your partner have to record one of the ways you sorted." Weslie said she wanted to sort their buttons by round and not round, and quickly sorted them on the paper. Bonnie

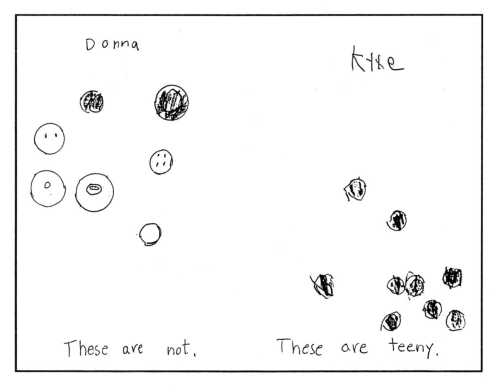

Donna and Kyle sorted their buttons by size.

then showed the children how to trace the buttons and color them in on the paper. She wrote *These are round* on one half and *These are not round* on the other.

"I'll help you write when you know what to say," she told the class. The children returned to the tables to work. They sorted in several ways: *These are teeny. These are not. These are colored buttons. These are white buttons.*

Some children sorted the buttons into more than two groups: *These have 4 holes. These have no holes. These have 2 holes.*

The children's interest in buttons was evident, and Bonnie planned to continue with further activities.

How Big Is a Foot?

Taught by Bonnie Tank and Lynne Zolli

In the book *How Big Is a Foot?* Rolf Myller tells the story of a King
who wanted to give his Queen a very special birthday present. This
amusing and ingenious story presents a dilemma that engages
children in thinking about measurement, ratio, and proportion.
Bonnie Tank read the book to a second-grade class in Jefferson
School in San Francisco, and Lynne Zolli introduced it to her third
graders at Jefferson School.

When the Queen's birthday approached, the King had a
problem: What could he give to someone who had everything? He
was pleased when he thought of having a bed made for her. At that
time, beds hadn't yet been invented, so the Queen certainly didn't
have one already.

To figure how big the bed should be, the King asked the Queen
to put on her new pajamas and lie down on the floor. Using his
paces, he measured and found that the bed must be six feet long
and three feet wide to be big enough to fit the Queen (including
her crown, which the Queen sometimes liked to wear to bed).

The apprentice who made the bed, however, was a good deal
smaller than the King. He carefully measured six of his feet for the
length and three of his feet for the width and built a beautiful bed,
but it was too short. The King was so angry that he had the
apprentice thrown into jail.

Sitting in the jail cell, the apprentice thought and thought and
finally realized what the problem was. He came up with a solution
and made a new bed. It was the right size for the Queen and was
ready just in time for her birthday. The King was so pleased that he
released the apprentice from jail and made him a royal prince.

Bonnie didn't read the entire story to the class but stopped once the
apprentice went to jail. She talked with the children about the

apprentice's problem and had them offer their suggestions. Bonnie then asked that they each write a letter to the apprentice and offer him advice. Their letters revealed different approaches to the problem.

Leslie explained what the apprentice should have done. She wrote: *Why was the bed so small? The king was very mad. Apprentice feet were very small! You should have measure with a ruler.*

Brandon put the responsibility on the King. He wrote: *I no why your in jail. Because your foot is to small. The bed is to small. The king should have measured with your foot.*

In his letter, Dominic also included advice about what the King should do. He wrote: *I think I know how to get you out of jail. Your feet are smaller than the king's feet. So tell the king that you messed up on the bed. And please could I have another chance at the bed. And ask him when you make it he has to measure the wood so it will be the right size.*

Max gave the apprentice specific advice about how to address the King. He wrote: *The bed whes [was] too small because yor feet*

In his letter, Dominic gave the apprentice advice for negotiating with the king.

October 16,

Dear Apprentice,

I think I know how to get you out of jail. Your feet are smaller than the king's feet. So tell the king that you messed up on the bed. And please could I have another chance at the bed. And ask him when you make it he has to measure the wood so it will be the right size.

Sincerely Dominic

10-18-15

Dear Apprentice,
The bed was to small because your feet were to small for the queen.
You can ask the king for one more chance.
But this time ask the king to use his feet.

Sincerly,
Bolan

1
2
3
4
5
6
Kings 6 feet

1
2
3
4
5
6
Your 6 feet

P.S. if this dasen't work have a nice time in the big house.

are *to small and the kings feet are bigger then yhour feet. Soew the idea is you ask the jaler to let you tik [talk] to the king and you can tell the king avry thing I told you. just sae I have too yose yor feet.*

Jennifer gave a mathematical solution that maintained the correct proportion between the length and the width. She wrote: *I am sorry that you are in jail, I think you sould make a new bed. The bed sould be ten feet long and five feet wide.*

The third graders included some different suggestions in their letters. Bolan, for example, wrote: *The bed was to small because your feet were to small for the queen. You can ask the king for one more chance. But this time ask the king to use his feet.* Bolan included a drawing to illustrate the comparison between six of the king's feet and six of the apprentice's feet. He also included a postscript: *P.S. if this doesn't work have a nice time in the big house.*

Matthew was one of
the children who
suggested using a
ruler.

10/18/1515

Dear Apprentice,

I am very sorry that you are in jail. The reason why the bed was too small was because your feet are too small and thats why it was too small. You can get a ruler at the nearst drug store and measure it.

Sincerely,
Matthew

1" 2" 3" 4" 5" 6" 7" 8"

and it keeps on going

In his letter, Jon gave advice and revealed his interest in Roman numerals. He wrote: *Show your king the difference in size. Now have your king step in paint and make a rectangle VI feet long and III feet wide. Now build the bed that size.*

Several of the children suggested the apprentice use a ruler. Matthew, for example, wrote: *I am very sorry that you are in jail. The reason why the bed was too small was because your feet are too small and thats why it was too small. You can get a ruler at the nearst drugstore and measure it.* He drew a picture of a ruler.

Eric wrote: *I think I can help you get out of jail if you invent a ruler. You ask for some wood that is 12 inch tall. And that will be a ruler.*

Instead of offering advice, Wanda explained the problem and concentrated her effort on her illustration. She wrote: *Your foot is to small to do like the king. And the kings foot is to big and your foot is to small to do it. That is your prublems.*

The book can be used to introduce the importance of standard units to communicate about measurements.

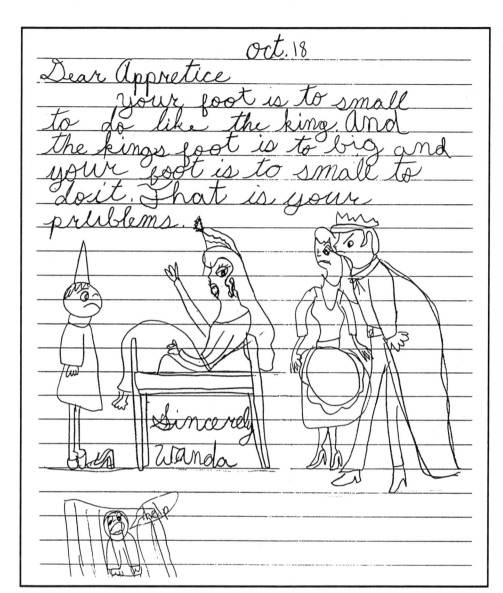

Oct. 18

Dear Appretice
            Your foot is to small
to do like the king. And
the kings foot is to big and
your foot is to small to
do it. That is your
pruiblems.

Sincerely
Wanda

PART 2
Additional Ideas

Alexander, Who Used to Be Rich Last Sunday

Judith Viorst

When Alexander's grandparents came to visit on Sunday, they gave him and his two brothers each a dollar. Alexander was rich, but not for long. There were all sorts of things to tempt him — bubble gum, some bets with his brothers, a snake rental, a garage sale, and more — and he just couldn't resist. By the end of the book, all Alexander had was bus tokens.

Begin by reading the book to the class in its entirety. Then read it again, stopping each time Alexander spends some of his dollar and asking the students to figure out how much he has left. Have the children figure mentally or give them coins to use; but in either case, have them explain their reasoning. You may also want to have the children record subtraction sentences to describe Alexander's expenditures.

As a follow-up activity, ask the students how they might spend a dollar. Start by having the class list things they would like to buy. Also have them estimate the prices of the things they suggest, and list these as well. Then have the children work individually or in pairs to plan how they might spend a dollar.

Anno's Counting House

Mitsumasa Anno

This wordless picture-story engages children in thinking about numbers through a clever and amusing game. Ten little people move one by one from a fully furnished home to an empty house next door. The book invites children to pick out which person has moved with which belongings. Cutout windows offer glimpses inside the new home, revealing just enough to pique children's curiosity.

Instructions about how to use this book are provided at the beginning of the story. The instructions advise providing counters in two different colors or sizes and suggesting to the children that they use one color or size to count the girls and the other for the boys. If possible, work with a small group of children. To begin, ask the students to put out counters to represent the little people in the house on the first page. Ask them how many people there are altogether, how many are boys, and how many are girls. As you turn the pages, have the children count how many people they see in the first house and predict how many they think there now are in the other house. At the end of the book, when the first house is empty, you can go through the book from back to front and have the children count as the people move back.

Don't miss the section at the end for parents and other adults. Anno writes about the kinds of early number experiences he feels are important for children, cites some of Piaget's findings, and addresses the value of this book in helping children acquire understanding. "Teaching by rote or force will not lead a child to better comprehension," he writes. "I'll be happy if this book helps children to think for themselves, following their own innate curiosity, and gives them a first experience of the immense beauty and intellectual pleasure that is to be found in the world of numbers."

Anno's Hat Tricks

Mitsumasa Anno and Akihiro Nozaki

There are 5 props in this inventive book: 3 red hats and 2 white hats. There are 4 characters: a hatter, Hannah, Tom, and the reader, called Shadowchild. The "tricks" in the book are logic problems pulled from the hatter's hat box. Shadowchild is shown throughout the book as a shadow, and each trick presents the challenge of figuring out whether he is wearing a red hat or a white hat.

The problems are sequenced from easy to difficult. In the first trick, the hatter takes 2 hats from his box, 1 red and 1 white. The illustration shows Tom wearing a red hat, and the children have to tell the color of Shadowchild's hat. When students offer solutions, be sure to have them explain their thinking. Keep the emphasis on having children clarify their ideas and convince each other. As the book progresses, the problems involve 3 hats and finally 5 hats. The later problems are challenging even for adults and therefore will be too difficult for the children. Stop when the children are no longer interested or engaged. Bring out the book later in the year or make it available for individual children.

A wonderful feature of all of Anno's books is that they help both adults and children learn. At the end of the book, a note to parents and other older readers addresses several aspects of logical reasoning, including the significance of the word *if* and the basics of binary logic. Also offered in this section is specific help with the most difficult problem in the book.

Anno's Mysterious Multiplying Jar
Masaichiro and Mitsumasa Anno

The story is about a beautiful blue-and-white porcelain jar whose contents magically change and multiply in a progression of beautiful images. The water in the jar becomes a sea in which there is an island. There are 2 countries on the island, 3 mountains in each country, and 4 walled kingdoms on each mountain. The story continues up to 10, and the resulting numbers become enormous.

Read the book to the class until you reach the question "But how many jars were in all the boxes together?" Tell the children the answer that's given — 3,628,800 jars — and write this number on the board. Then begin reading the book again, this time stopping to have children use calculators to verify the number of mountains, kingdoms, villages, houses, and so on, there are altogether. Having the students say the answers aloud provides them practice with reading large numbers. Show them the pages of dots at the end of the book that illustrate the answers.

As in all his books, Anno provides a mathematical afterword. In this section, he explains factorial numbers and describes their usefulness.

The Doorbell Rang
Pat Hutchins

The doorbell rang just when Sam and Victoria were about to share the dozen cookies Ma had baked. It was Hannah and Tom from next door, and Ma invited them to share the cookies. Before they began to eat, however, the doorbell rang again, and then again.

Finally, there were 12 hungry children with 1 cookie each. But the doorbell rang once more, bringing the book to a surprising and satisfying ending.

As you read the story to the class, stop each time there is an opportunity for the students to figure out how to share the cookies. For example, at the beginning of the story, Sam and Victoria announced that if they shared the cookies on the plate, they each would get 6. Ask the children to use that information to figure out how many cookies Ma had baked altogether. Have children explain their thinking, and ask the class to report all the different strategies they used to find the answer.

Continue reading until Ma invites Hannah and Tom to share the cookies. Have the class figure out how many cookies each child will then have. Again, keep the emphasis on the children's reasoning rather than merely on their solutions. Once all who are interested have presented their thinking, turn the page to verify the answer.

Continue reading the story, but stop each time new children arrive. Ask the students to figure out the number of cookies each child gets, and have them discuss their thinking

The story also provides the opportunity to introduce or reinforce the appropriate symbolism for division. Record each sharing problem on the chalkboard:

$$12 \div 2 = 6$$
$$12 \div 4 = 3$$
$$12 \div 6 = 2$$
$$12 \div 12 = 1$$

Point out to the students that each mathematical sentence can be read in several ways. Model with one sentence, and then have students do the same for the others. For example:

12 divided by 2 equals 6.
12 divided into 2 groups gives 6 in each group.
12 cookies shared between 2 children gives 6 cookies each.

Eight Hands Round

Ann Whitford Paul

This alphabet book uses the names of early American patchwork patterns for its letters, beginning with Anvil and Buggy Wheel, and ending with Yankee Puzzle and Zigzag. The quilts and the individual patches are illustrated in colorful detail. Also, the text tells how patchwork-making began, where people got their ideas for designs, and how the patterns were named.

Have the children examine the different shapes used in the patterns. To focus them more specifically, have them talk about each pattern and describe whether it's made only from squares, only from triangles, or from both squares and triangles. Distribute 2-inch squares in two different colors of construction paper for the students to make their own designs. Instruct them to use only 9 squares, cut any or all of them into triangles, explore the different arrangements they can make, and finally choose a design to paste on drawing paper. Have the children post their patterns.

To extend the activity, have the students write descriptions of their patterns. Model this with a pattern you've made or one from the book. Tell how many squares and triangles it has, what's in the corners, and describe any particular horizontal, vertical, or diagonal patterns. As you describe, write words on the board that may be of use to the children as they write their descriptions, such as *corner, middle, top, bottom, horizontal, vertical,* and *diagonal.* To help the students get started, write the following on the board:

My pattern has ___ squares and ___ triangles.

Once the children have written their descriptions, have them take turns reading them aloud while their classmates try to identify the matching pattern.

The Fine Round Cake

Arnica Esterl

In this variation of the Gingerbread Boy story, an old woman put a fine round cake into the oven to bake. When her hungry little boy opened the oven door to peek inside, the cake jumped out and rolled right out the door. It was chased, unsuccessfully, by the boy and his parents, 2 well-diggers, 2 girls with red berries, a bear, and a wolf. Finally, a fox used her wits to snap up the cake.

The book can be used to initiate a discussion and investigation of the sorts of things that do and do not roll. Have students brainstorm a list of objects to test. Test objects you have in the classroom and invite the children to bring things from home to try. Talk about the different characteristics of objects that can and can't roll.

A bonus: The inside front and back covers of the book are illustrated with a repeating pattern of suns, moons, and stars. Show the pattern to the children and ask them to describe the patterns they notice. Take this opportunity to introduce and reinforce words such as *pattern, repeating, diagonal, vertical,* and *horizontal.*

Grandfather Tang's Story
Ann Tompert

The book opens with Grandfather Tang and Little Soo sitting under a peach tree making different shapes with their tangram puzzles. Little Soo requested a story about fox fairies, and Grandfather Tang complied. He arranged each of their puzzles into a fox and told the story of Chou and Wu Ling, fox fairies who could change their shapes. Throughout this dramatic story-within-a-story, the different shapes are illustrated with tangram designs.

The tangram illustrations in the book include a rabbit, dog, squirrel, hawk, turtle, crocodile, goldfish, goose, and lion. After you read the story, have children use the tangram pieces to make various shapes, following the patterns in the book or inventing shapes of their own. Also, the students can write their own stories and illustrate them with their own tangram constructions.

The Half-Birthday Party
Charlotte Pomerantz

Daniel was so impressed when his six-month-old sister, Katie, stood on her own for the first time that he decided to give her a half-birthday party. He invited his parents, his grandmother, and the neighbors and asked each to bring Katie half a present. "You have to tell a whole story about the half present," he added. Daniel got so involved in his plans that he forgot to get a half present of his own. But he came up with an ingenious solution.

This book can be used to introduce investigations about birthdays, the calendar, and the idea of halves. For a birthday-related problem, have the children figure out how many half-birthdays they've each had. In a class discussion, have volunteers explain how they arrived at their answers. To engage the students in thinking about the calendar, ask them to figure out on which day of the year their half-birthday falls. Have them share their thinking in a class discussion. For this investigation, it's useful to have calendars available for the children to use.

The story provides several examples of halves. Katie's gifts included half a pair of slippers, half a poem, and half a birthday cake. Ask the children to name other things that could be divided for half presents. Then have them think of things that could not be divided into halves, such as balloons or marbles. Compile the children's ideas on class lists.

How Many Feet in the Bed?

Diane Johnston Hamm

This bright and cozy counting book begins with a little girl asking her father, one morning when he wakes up, "How many feet are in the bed?" He answered, "I thought there were two." But then the little girl climbed in, followed by brother Tom, baby Jane, and then her mother. Each time, they figured out how many feet were in the bed, and they continued their figuring as the bed emptied two by two.

The book can be used to initiate several possible problems. One is to have the children figure out how many feet there are in the class. Ask that they show their work and explain their reasoning. Having students present their methods to the class helps reinforce that there is more than one way to solve a problem.

If this problem is too difficult for your students, give a problem with smaller numbers. In her pre-first class in Edison, Washington, Leslie Salkeld gathered 6 children around a table during reading time. She asked them how many feet they thought were under the table. She also asked them not to peek but to figure it out first. After sharing their ideas, the children used blocks, counted by twos, and finally looked under the table to check.

For a variation on the problems presented in the book, introduce the possibility that a pet dog or cat could also be in bed. If there were 10 feet in bed, for example, there could be 5 people, or 3 people and 1 cat, or 1 person, 1 cat, and 1 dog. Have the children figure different possibilities for 12 feet in a bed.

If You Look Around You

Fulvio Testa

The pixie-like children, their romping pets, and many toys in this book pique children's interest and stimulate their imagination about shapes. A line is described as a dog's leash, a square as a magician's handkerchief, a cylinder as Teddy Bear's drum, and more. The illustrations encourage children's observation and discussion of point, line, triangle, circle, square, cylinder, cone, cube, and sphere.

Talk with the class about each of the geometric shapes and ask for other ideas to describe them. Have students identify objects in the class that provide examples. Suggest to the children that they make their own books about the geometric shapes modeled after *If You Look Around You*. Have them choose their own objects, write sentences, and make illustrations.

You may want to have all the students contribute to a class book. After reading the book twice to a class of first graders in Houston, Stephanie Sheffield asked the children to recall the shapes in the book. She listed on the board the shapes they remembered and then went through the book to see which ones they had missed. Considering the shapes one by one, Stephanie had the children think of objects in the world for each. She then had each child choose one shape, illustrate it with an object, and write a sentence about it. Stephanie compiled the children's papers into a class book.

You may want to enlist ideas from parents as well. Before the children choose their shapes, you may want to duplicate the list of ideas you've recorded on the board and send it home for homework so that parents can help think of other objects. Homework assignments such as this one can help educate parents about their children's math learning. Back in class, the students can report the additions and then make their choices.

Louise Builds a House

Louise Pfanner

Louise gives her reasons for the useful and whimsical features she builds into her house. She builds a flat roof to fly kites from, big windows to read in, small windows to paint on, and a tower to watch the planets and comets from. She includes a moat and a drawbridge, as well as arches, steps, gardens, beehives, and a plot of small trees. The construction shown page by page is described in simple words and accompanied by engaging illustrations.

Ann Carlyle, who teaches kindergarten in Goleta, California, has found the story useful for motivating construction projects. After reading the book, she talked with the children about other sorts of things Louise could build and suggested they try some themselves in the block center. The students' constructions included a castle, a zoo, several houses, a camera, a pirate ship, and more. As they built, Ann asked the children to describe their constructions and explain their design choices. She was especially pleased that the book served to attract more girls to the block center.

Some children were able to draw their constructions, and Ann made sketches for the others. She recorded the children's descriptions on all the drawings and posted them. (One year, Ann took photographs of the children's constructions and posted them with captions the children dictated.)

Note: At the end of the book, Louise announces her plans for when the house is finished. "I will give it to my sister," she says, "and then I think I'll build a sailboat." You can find out about her new project in the companion book *Louise Builds a Boat*.

The Midnight Farm

Reeve Lindberg

In this beautifully illustrated book, a mother and son tour a farm at midnight. A counting rhyme searches out the farm's wild and domestic animals — 1 old dog, 2 white cats, a family of 3 raccoons, 4 farm geese, 5 horses stamping their feet, 6 standing cows, 7 fat sheep, 8 little chicks, 9 quiet deer, and 10 small field mice. The illustrations suggest a quiet stillness that presents darkness as warm and comforting.

This book can be used for the same sort of investigation suggested in Part 1 for *1 Hunter* and *One Gorilla*. Present the students with the problem of figuring out how many animals the boy and his mother saw altogether. For problems with simpler numbers that also engage the children in sorting and classifying the animals, ask them how many of the animals have feathers, how many are wild animals, how many are welcome inside the house, how many have two feet each, how many have long tails, and so on.

Ocean Parade

Patricia MacCarthy

Shimmering schools of fantastical fish swim through the batik paintings in this book. The first two-page spread shows 1 big fish and 2 little fish; the second spread shows 3 flat fish, 4 thin fish, and 5 fat fish; the third shows 6 long eels, 7 short fish, and an octopus with 8 arms. The counting continues by ones to 20 green sea horses, and then jumps to counting by tens, from 30 little purple fish up to 100 silver fish.

To focus on mental computation, talk about the number of fish on each two-page spread. For example, one spread has 11 tiny fish, 12 patterned fish, and 13 plain fish. Ask the children to figure out how many there are altogether and have them share their methods. Also, discuss the descriptions of the different fish and have the children discuss the attributes of the groupings on each spread, such as size, length, and color.

Marge Genolio had her class of first graders in San Francisco replicate *Ocean Parade* in a big-book format. Each group of students took responsibility for a two-page spread. They figured out how many fish they needed and decided how to divide the work of cutting out and decorating the fish. They used 18-by-24-inch paper for each spread, watercolor sponged backgrounds, and crayon-resist drawings for the fish.

Opt: An Illusionary Tale

Arline and Joseph Baum

Opt is a kingdom full of optical illusions that prove just how often our eyes can deceive us. The book is brightly illustrated and leads the reader from the wall outside the castle past the castle guard, royal messenger, and trumpeters to the royal art gallery, great hall, pavilion, and tower. A question on each page challenges the reader to consider an optical illusion.

The illusions in the book challenge perceptions of color, shape, and size, and engage children in examining and comparing geometric shapes. It's best to introduce the book to pairs or small groups of children so that they can inspect the drawings closely. Have the children describe what they think and, if possible, find a way to test their predictions. The illusions in which the sizes of objects are compared are especially useful for giving children the opportunity to use measurement skills to check their predictions. At the end of the book, the questions are answered, the illusions are explained, and directions are given for children to make their own illusions.

Sea Squares

Joy N. Hulme

In imaginative rhymes with colorful illustrations, this book combines counting with learning about square numbers. Using an ocean theme, the book begins with 1 whale that has 1 spout and 1 tail. It moves to 2 white gulls with 2 eyes each, making 4 eyes to watch the beach; 3 fish with 3 stripes each, making 9 stripes altogether; and on up to 10 squids, each having 10 tentacles. Information about the sea life shown is presented at the end of the book.

As you read the book to the children, some may be interested in predicting the numbers on the next page. Ask children to think and talk about the relationships between the pairs of numbers. Some are easier for children than others. For example, because most children have learned to count by fives, they are better prepared to explain why 5 lilies, each with 5 fronds, results in 25 fronds altogether.

Use tiles, cubes, or counters to interpret the pairs of numbers geometrically. Demonstrate with the page that shows 4 seals with 4 flippers each. Show the children how to arrange 16 counters into a square array and tell them that 16 is therefore called a square number. Have the children check that the larger of each of the other pairs of numbers is also a square number.

The Shapes Game

Paul Rogers

This book introduces young children to a variety of shapes. Each two-page spread presents a different shape through a riddle and a dazzlingly colored picture. The shapes include squares, circles, triangles, ovals, crescents, rectangles, diamonds, spirals, and stars. Each "I spy" riddle mentions several different real-world objects. For example, the rectangle riddle begins:

I spy a doorway, A picture on the wall,
A window shape, a cage shape,
A look! — this-very-page shape —
These shapes we call ... rectangles.

As you show each page to the children, have them describe all the different examples of the shape in the illustration. For each shape they spy, encourage them to tell its color, size, and position on the page. To follow up the book discussion, have the students explore objects in the classroom and around the school. Also, take walks in the neighborhood, each time having the children look for examples of one particular shape.

Shapes, Shapes, Shapes

Tana Hoban

This collection of Tana Hoban's colorful and intriguing photographs helps children see that wherever they are, inside or outside, there are shapes to discover. The book initiates the discovery by providing a list of some shapes to look for in the photographs: arcs, circles, hearts, hexagons, ovals, parallelograms, rectangles, squares, stars, trapezoids, and triangles.

The photographs show children and adults engaged in a variety of activities — sailing a boat, bicycling, shopping, doing laundry, playing instruments, painting, and more. The settings vary and include city and country scenes. Talk about each photograph with the students, asking them to notice and identify as many shapes as they can. After examining the photographs in the book, have the children look for and describe the shapes they see in the classroom, around the school, or on walks in the neighborhood.

The Tangram Magician

Lisa Campbell Ernst and Lee Ernst

The magician in this book dreamed of many worlds. He wanted to fly high above the earth and soar with the wind, so he became a bird. He longed to see the bottom of the ocean and the top of a mountain, and so became a fish and a mountain goat. Each of his transformations is illustrated with the 7 pieces of the tangram puzzle. The book comes with vinyl stickers of the puzzle pieces.

In the story, the magician also became a swan, a camel, a sailboat, a house, a tea set, a dog, and a cat — all illustrated with the tangram pieces. Then he rested and wondered what to become next. He thought about becoming a lion, a tree, a rooster, a snake, a raccoon, or a goose. The book ends by asking the reader to help him decide, a perfect invitation to have the children use tangram pieces to explore shapes on their own. Have the students each experiment making different designs with the tangram pieces. Also have them glue or trace their pieces to make the design that pleased them most. These can be posted or assembled into a book.

Ten Little Rabbits

Virginia Grossman and Sylvia Long

Weaving, fishing, and storytelling are all part of this counting book that celebrates Native American traditions. The book presents

1 lonely traveler, 2 graceful dancers, 3 busy messengers, and on up to 10 sleepy weavers. Each number introduces a facet of traditional Native American culture — Pueblo corn dances, Navajo weaving, and others.

Use this book for the same sort of investigation suggested in Part I for *1 Hunter* and *One Gorilla* and have the students figure out how many rabbits there are altogether. Also, the information at the end of the book is valuable for helping the children learn about Native American customs.

What Comes in 2's, 3's, and 4's?

Suzanne Aker

This book focuses on things that come in groups of 2, 3, and 4. It begins with a picture of a boy, pointing out that there are 2 each of eyes, ears, arms, hands, and legs. It then continues looking at 2's with the handles on the sink, pieces of bread in a sandwich, wings on birds and airplanes, and so on. The same sort of treatment is presented for 3's and 4's.

The book is a natural way to introduce the idea of multiplication. After reading the book to the children, have them think of other things that come in 2's, 3's, and 4's. Post a piece of chart paper for each number and record their suggestions. Then have the students work in small groups and think of things that come in 5's, 6's, 7's, and so on up to 12's. The items of their lists can be used to generate explorations of multiples. For example, on 1 bird there are 2 wings, on 2 birds there are 4 wings, on 3 there are 6, etc. Or have children write and solve word problems. For example, if a chair has 4 legs, how many legs are there on 5 chairs?

BIBLIOGRAPHY

Aker, Suzanne. *What Comes in 2's, 3's, and 4's?* New York, NY: Simon and Schuster Books for Young Readers, 1990.

Anno, Masaichiro and Mitsumasa. *Anno's Mysterious Multiplying Jar.* New York, NY: Philomel Books, 1983.

Anno, Mitsumasa. *Anno's Counting House.* New York, NY: Philomel Books, 1982.

Anno, Mitsumasa, and Akihiro Nozaki. *Anno's Hat Tricks.* New York, NY: Philomel Books, 1985.

Baum, Arline and Joseph. *Opt: An Illusionary Tale.* New York, NY: Puffin Books, 1987.

Carle, Eric. *Rooster's Off to See the World.* Saxonville, MA: Picture Book Studio Ltd., 1972.

Crews, Donald. *Ten Black Dots.* New York, NY: Greenwillow Books, 1986.

Dee, Ruby. *Two Ways to Count to Ten.* New York, NY: Henry Holt and Company, Inc., 1988.

Ernst, Lisa Campbell, and Lee Ernst. *The Tangram Magician.* New York, NY: Harry N. Abrams, Inc., 1990.

Esterl, Arnica. *The Fine Round Cake.* New York, NY: Four Winds Press, 1991.

Geringer, Laura. *A Three Hat Day.* New York, NY: Harper & Row, 1985.

Grossman, Virginia, and Sylvia Long. *Ten Little Rabbits.* San Francisco, CA: Chronicle Books, 1991.

Hamm, Diane Johnston. *How Many Feet in the Bed?* New York, NY: Simon & Schuster Books for Young Readers, 1991.

Hoban, Tana. *Shapes, Shapes, Shapes.* New York, NY: Greenwillow Books, 1986.

Hulme, Joy N. *Sea Squares.* New York, NY: Hyperion Books for Children, 1991.

Hutchins, Pat. *The Doorbell Rang.* New York, NY: Greenwillow Books, 1986.

Hutchins, Pat. *1 Hunter.* New York, NY: Mulberry Books, 1982.

Lindbergh, Reeve. *The Midnight Farm.* New York, NY: Dial Books for Young Readers, 1987.

MacCarthy, Patricia. *Ocean Parade.* New York, NY: Dial Books for Young Readers, 1990.

Mahy, Margaret. *17 Kings and 42 Elephants.* New York, NY: Dial Books for Young Readers, 1987.

Morozumi, Atsuko. *One Gorilla.* New York, NY: Farrar, Straus & Giroux, 1990.

Myller, Rolf. *How Big Is a Foot?* New York, NY: Dell Publishing, 1962.

Paul, Ann Whitford. *Eight Hands Round.* New York, NY: Harper Collins Publishers, 1991.

Pfanner, Louise. *Louise Builds a Boat.* New York, NY: Orchard Books, 1989.

Pfanner, Louise. *Louise Builds a House.* New York, NY: Orchard Books, 1987.

Pomerantz, Charlotte. *The Half-Birthday Party*. New York, NY: Clarion Books, 1984.

Reid, Margarette S. *The Button Box*. New York, NY: Dutton Children's Books, 1990.

Rogers, Paul. *The Shapes Game*. New York, NY: Henry Holt and Company, 1989.

Silverstein, Shel. *Where the Sidewalk Ends*. New York, NY: Harper & Row, 1974.

Testa, Fulvio. *If You Look Around You*. New York, NY: Dial Books for Young Readers, 1982.

Tompert, Ann. *Grandfather Tang's Story*. New York, NY: Crown Publishers, Inc., 1990.

Viorst, Judith. *Alexander, Who Used to Be Rich Last Sunday*. New York, NY: Atheneum, 1978.

Wilder, Laura Ingalls. *Little House in the Big Woods*. New York, NY: Harper & Row, 1932.